"中国民间武术经典"丛书
Chinese Folk Wushu Classic Series

中国武术入门之
初级剑术

THE BASIC FORM OF CHINESE WUSHU
PRIMARY SWORD PLAY

李素玲 郭笑丹 主编

Chief Editor Li Suling Guo Xiaodan

纪秋云 著

Compiler Ji Qiuyun

杨少华 译

Translator Yang Shaohua

海燕出版社
PETREL PUBLISHING HOUSE

河南电子音像出版社
HENAN ELECTRONIC & AUDIOVISUAL PRESS

图书在版编目(CIP)数据

中国武术入门之初级剑术：汉英对照 / 纪秋云编著；
杨少华译. — 郑州：海燕出版社，2008.8
（中国民间武术经典）
ISBN 978-7-5350-3786-2

Ⅰ.中…　Ⅱ.①纪…②杨…　Ⅲ.剑术（武术）
—中国—汉、英　Ⅳ.G852.24

中国版本图书馆CIP数据核字（2008）第077975号

中国武术入门之初级剑术
THE BASIC FORM OF CHINESE WUSHU PRIMARY SWORD PLAY

出版发行：海燕出版社　河南电子音像出版社
Publish: Petrel Publishing House　Henan Electronic & Audiovisual Press

地址：河南省郑州市经五路66号
Add: No.66 Jingwu Road of Zhengzhou, Henan Province, China

邮编：450002
Pc: 450002

电话：+86-371-65720922
Tel: +86-371-65720922

传真：+86-371-65733354
Fax: +86-371-65733354

印刷：河南地质彩色印刷厂
开本：850×1168　1/16
印张：3.5
字数：42千字
印数：1-1 000册
版次：2008年8月郑州第1版
印次：2008年8月第1次印刷
书号：ISBN 978-7-5350-3786-2
定价：20.50元

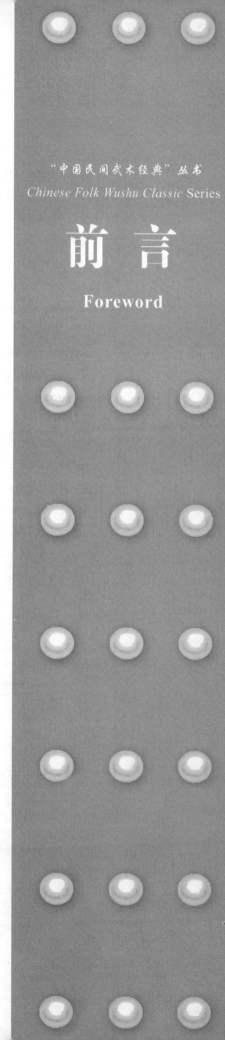

"中国民间武术经典"丛书
Chinese Folk Wushu Classic Series

前 言

Foreword

百集"中国民间武术经典"光盘在国内外发行之后，引起巨大的反响，深受广大武术界同行的好评，特别是海外广大武术爱好者慕名而来，拜师求学者络绎不绝，并都希望看到与之相配套的文字教材。应广大读者的要求，我们以中英文对照形式编写了这套"中国民间武术经典"丛书，以帮助广大武术爱好者学习和了解博大精深的中华武术文化。

中华武术源远流长。本套丛书详细介绍了少林、太极、峨嵋、武当、形意等诸多门派，包括内家和外家，近300余种拳法和武功绝活儿，是目前我国向国内外推介的最权威、最系统、最全面的武术文化精品。

"中国民间武术经典"丛书采用图文教材与影视教材相结合的立体教学手段，全方位地展现中华武术文化精髓。每个套路邀请代表当今最高水平的全国武术冠军、正宗流派传人以及著名武术专家进行技术演练和教学示范，保证学习者获取原汁原味的技法。

在丛书编写过程中，得到中国武术协会副主席王玉龙先生的关照支持，我们表示衷心感谢！参加本丛书校对工作的人员有张青川、邵佳、王浩、邵倩、韩晓宁等，在此一并致谢！

The 100 sets of *Chinese Folk Wushu Classic* compact disc has received great attention home and abroad since its publication. Most foreign Wushu lovers hope to get the written teaching materials attached to it. We have prepared this series of *Chinese Folk Wushu Classic* to help them understand the Chinese martial art and Chinese culture.

Chinese Wushu has a long history which is profound in content. This series have details on Shaolin, Taiji, Emei, etc. Including internal school and external school, nearly 300 species of the fist position and military accomplishments. They are the most authoritative, systemic and comprehensive of Wushu essence.

Chinese Folk Wushu Classic Series use graphic and video materials to demonstrate the best of the Chinese Wushu. For each routine, we invited the national Wushu champions, the orthodox heirs and famous Wushu experts who represent the highest level to conduct the technical trainings and the teaching demonstrations to guarantee the original techniques of these routines for the learners.

We express our heartfelt gratitude to Wang Yulong, vice-chairman of Chinese Wushu Association for his support and help in the process of compiling these books. We also thank Zhang Qingchuan, Shao Jia, Wang Hao, Shao Qian, Han Xiaoning for their careful work in revising our books. Thanks a lot!

编者

Editor

二〇〇七年七月大暑

July 2007 Summer

"中国民间武术经典"丛书

Chinese Folk Wushu Classic Series

编写委员会 **Writing Committee**

主 任 Director

高明星（河南电子音像出版社社长、编审）

Gao Mingxing, Proprietor, Copy Editor of Henan Electronic &

Audiovisual Press

副主任 Assistant Director

李　惠（河南省体育局武术运动管理中心副主任）

Li Hui, Assistant Director of Wushu Center of Henan Province Physical

Education Office

杨东军（河南电子音像出版社总编辑、编审）

Yang Dongjun, Chief Editor, Copy Editor of Henan Electronic &

Audiovisual Press

段嫩芝（河南电子音像出版社编审）

Duan Nenzhi, Copy Editor of Henan Electronic & Audiovisual Press

李素玲（江南大学体育学院副教授）

Li Suling, Associate Professor of Institute of Physical Education

of Jiangnan University

委 员 Commissioner

马　雷（公安部中国前卫搏击协会秘书长）

Ma Lei, Secretary-general of Chinese Advance Guard

Defy Association of Ministry of Public Security

郭笑丹（河南龙腾多媒体技术制作有限公司经理）

Guo Xiaodan, General Manager of Henan Dragon Television

Production Company

吴兴强 （重庆大学体育学院副教授）

Wu Biqiang, Associate Professor of Institute of Physical Education

of Chongqing University

凌长鸣 （江苏信息职业技术学院体育部主任、副教授）

Ling Changming, Sports Department Deputy Director, Associate Professor

Technology College of Information Vocational of Jiangsu Province

杨　琦 （江苏省武术协会常务理事、无锡市体育运动学校副校长）

Yang Qi, Managing Director of Wushu Association Jiangsu Province

Vice-Chancellor of Sports School Wuxi City

总策划 Chief Producer

高明星 Gao Mingxing

责任编辑　Editors in Charge

赵　建 Zhao Jian

"中国民间武术经典"丛书

Chinese Folk Wushu Classic Series

作者名单 Author List

主　编　Chief Editor

李素玲　　　郭笑丹

Li Suling　　Guo Xiaodan

副主编　Assistant Editor

李　惠　　　贾大伟　　　毛景宇

Li Hui　　　Jia Dawei　　Mao Jingyu

编　委　Members of the Editorial Board（以姓氏笔画为序 Name of a Sequence of Strokes）

马雷	代小平	丛亚贤	纪秋云	刘海科
Ma Lei	Dai Xiaoping	Cong Yaxian	Ji Qiuyun	Liu Haike
乔熛	何义凡	许定国	杨华	杨玉峰
Qiao Biao	He Yifan	Xu Dingguo	Yang Hua	Yang Yufeng
张亚东	张学谦	张希珍	高秀明	袁剑龙
Zhang Yadong	Zhang Xueqian	Zhang Xizhen	Gao Xiuming	Yuan Jianlong
潘艳	孙永文	郑爱民	杜金山	李秀娟
Pan Yan	Sun Yongwen	Zheng Aimin	Du Jinshan	Li Xiujuan
李瑞				
Li Rui				

视频示范　Video Performer

刘　铮　Liu Zheng

动作示范　Illustrators

侯　雯　　　赵阳阳

Hou Wen　　Zhao Yangyang

摄　影　Photographers

贾大伟　Jia Dawei　　　林伟峰　Lin Weifeng

目 录

第一章　概述

OVERVIEW

第一节　基本技术
BASIC TECHNIQUE

一、手型
Hands Forms

1. 拳 Fist

五指攥紧，拳面要平，拇指压于食指、中指第二指节上。（序图1）

Clenching five fingers, fist-face is plane, thumb presses on the index finger and middle finger. (Picture 1)

序图1

2. 掌 Palm

拇指内屈，其余四指伸直并拢向后伸张。（序图2）

Bend inside thumb and the other four fingers upright. (Picture 2)

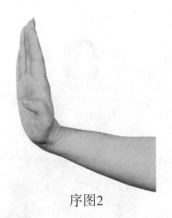

序图2

3. 勾 Hook

屈腕，五指撮拢。（序图3）

Wrist bends and five fingers gather.
(Picture 3)

序图3

二、步型
Stances

1. 弓步 Bow step

前脚微内扣，全脚掌着地，屈
膝，大腿水平，膝部与脚尖垂直；
另一腿挺膝伸直，脚尖里扣斜向前
方，全脚掌着地（两脚间距三脚半
左右）。（序图4）

Front tiptoe inward and sole supports,
thigh flatly and knee vertical; the other leg
is straight, tiptoe inward oblique forwards,
(the distance between feet keeps three and
a half feet-length). (Picture 4)

序图4

2. 马步 Horse-riding Step

两脚左右开立，脚尖微内扣，屈
膝半蹲，大腿接近水平。（序图5）

Stand apart, tiptoe inward, squat
knees, thighs flatly. (Picture 5)

序图5

3. 仆步 Crouch Step

一腿屈膝全蹲，大腿和小腿靠紧，全脚掌着地，膝与脚尖稍外展；另一腿平铺接近地面，全脚掌着地，脚尖内扣。（序图6）

One leg fully squats with thigh and calf together, a whole foot down, knee and tiptoe slightly outward; another leg is straight close to ground with the whole foot down and tiptoe inward deduction. (Picture 6)

序图6

4. 虚步 Empty Step

后脚尖斜向前，屈膝半蹲，大腿接近水平，全脚掌着地；前腿微屈，脚面绷紧，脚尖虚点地面。（序图7）

Back tiptoe forward, knee squats a half, the thigh flatly slightly, foot down steadily; front leg bends slightly with foot-back straight and tiptoe on the ground. (Picture 7)

序图7

5. 歇步 Cross-legged Step

两腿交叉，屈膝全蹲，前脚全脚掌着地，脚尖外展；后脚脚后跟离地，臀部外侧紧贴小腿。（序图8）

Cross legs and squat knees completely, the front sole touches ground with tiptoe outward; back heel the outside of buttocks sticks to calf. (Picture 8)

序图8

6. 坐盘 Cross-legged Sitting Position

两腿交叉叠拢下坐，臀部和右腿的大小腿外侧及脚面均着地；左腿的大腿靠近胸部。（序图9）

Legs under cross-sitting, buttocks and right leg touches ground; the thigh of left leg is near the chest. (Picture 9)

序图9

7. 丁步 T-stance

两腿并拢半蹲，一脚全脚掌着地，另一脚脚尖点地，靠在支撑脚内侧，支撑腿大腿成水平。（序图10）

Legs together and half-squat, one foot on the ground, the other tiptoe points on the ground, lean on inside of the supporting leg, the thigh of supporting leg keeps flatly. (Picture 10)

序图10

8. 横裆步 Horizontal Crotch Step

两脚左右开立，约同弓步宽，全脚掌着地，脚尖向前方。（序图11）

Legs apart, about the same width as bow step, with the whole foot down and tiptoe forward. (Picture 11)

序图11

1. 拳法 Fist Techniques

（1）抱拳：两臂垂直上提，同时两手变拳抱于腰间，拳心向上。（序图12、序图13）

Hold fist: arms rise up, at the same time hands into fists at waist, fist-palm upward. (Picture 12, Picture 13)

（2）冲拳（前冲、侧冲、上冲）：拳从腰间旋臂向前快速击出，力达拳面。侧冲、上冲要求同此，唯方向不同。（序图14）

Thrust fist (thrust forward, thrust side, thrust up): Punch from the waist, at the same time recoil naturally and slightly bend arm with strength to fist-face. Thrust sideward and thrust up as the same requirements of this, but in different directions. (Picture 14)

（3）抄拳：臂微屈，拳自下向前上方抄起击打，高不过头，拳背向前，力达拳面。（序图15）

Uppercut fist: Arm bends slightly, punches forward from down to up, fist no higher than head, fist-back forward, power to fist-face. (Picture 15)

序图12

序图13

序图14

序图15

（4）栽拳：臂由屈到伸，自上向下或由前向下栽。速度要快，前臂内旋，拳眼向内，臂伸直或微屈，力达拳面。（序图16）

Plunge fist downward: Arm moves from bending to extension, from upward to downward or from forward crashed. Faster rate, forearm rotation inward, fist-eye inward, arm straight or slightly curly, powers to fist face. (Picture 16)

序图16

（5）架拳：一拳架于额前上方，肘微屈成弧形，臂与前额相距约15厘米，拳心向上。（序图17）

Block fist upper: One fist rises over his forehead, elbow slightly curly, arm and forehead apart about 15cm with fist-center upward. (Picture 17)

序图17

（6）劈拳：拳自上向下快速劈击，臂伸直，力达拳轮。抡臂劈击时臂要抡圆。（序图18）

Chop fist: Chop fist downward swiftly, arm straightens with power to fist-face. Try best to move into a round to punch. (Picture 18)

序图18

2. 掌法 Palm Techniques

（1）推掌：掌由腰间旋臂向前立掌推击，臂微屈，速度要快，力达掌根或掌外沿。（序图19、序图20）

Push palm: Push palm forward quickly with arm twisting from waist, arm bent slightly, powers to palm-root or palm edge. (Picture 19, Picture 20)

序图19

（2）插掌：臂由屈到伸，直腕向下（向前）插掌，力达指尖。（序图21）

Thrust palm: Shift arm from bent to straight, thrust downward (forward) with wrist straight, power to finger-tip. (Picture 21)

序图20

（3）砍掌：臂由屈到伸，仰掌向左，俯掌向右击打，力达掌外沿。（序图22）

Cut palm: Shift arm from bent to straight, palm-up punches leftward, palm-down punches rightward, power to palm-edge. (Picture 22)

序图21

序图22

（4）按掌：自上向下按，手心向下，力达掌心。（序图23）

Press palm: Press palm up to down with palm-heart downward, power punches to palm-heart. (Picture 23)

序图23

3. 肘法　Elbow Techniques

（1）顶肘：屈肘握拳，拳心向下，肘尖前顶或侧顶，力达肘尖。（序图24）

Elbow strike: Bend elbow and hold fist with fist-heart downward, elbow-tip pushes forward or sideward, power punches to elbow-tip. (Picture 24)

序图24

（2）盘肘：手臂平举，拳心向下，前臂由外向内盘肘。（序图25）

Bend elbow: Arm rises levelly with fist-heart downward, bend elbow from outer to inner. (Picture 25)

（3）格肘（里格、外格）：前臂上屈，拳心向里，力在前臂，向

序图25

序图26

内横拨为里格，向外横拨为外格。
（序图26）

Parry elbow (parry inside, parry outside): Bend forearm up, fist-heart inside, the strength in the forearm, parry outside or inside. (Picture 26)

（4）横击肘：肘关节屈，弧形向前，屈臂平击，力达肘尖和前臂外侧。（序图27）

Crosscut elbow: Bend elbow, curve forward to punch, power punches to elbow-tip and forearm outside. (Picture 27)

序图27

四、腿法
Leg Techniques

1. 曲伸性腿法 Flexor and Extend Leg Techniques

（1）弹腿：支撑腿直立或稍屈，另一腿由屈到伸向前弹击，高不过腰，脚面绷平稍内扣，力达脚尖。（序图28、序图29）

Flip kicking leg: The supporting leg stands straight or bends slightly, and the other leg flips forward kicking, waist high, foot-face smooth and buckle in slightly, power punches to tiptoe. Leg flips in place and then rebounds naturally. (Picture 28, Picture 29)

序图28

序图29

（2）蹬腿：支撑腿直立或稍屈，另一腿由屈到伸，脚尖勾起用脚跟猛力蹬出，高不过胸，低不过腰。（序图30、序图31）

Kick heel: The supporting leg stands straight or bends slightly, the other leg kicks with heel, with the tiptoe hooking, no higher than chest and no lower than waist not as low as waist. (Picture 30, Picture 31)

序图30

序图31

（3）踹腿（高踹、低踹、侧踹）：支撑腿直立或稍屈，另一腿由屈到伸，脚尖勾起内扣，用脚底猛力踹出。高踹与腰平；低踹与膝平；侧踹时上身斜倾，脚高与腰平。（序图32～序图34）

Sole side kick (high-kick, low-kick, side-kick): The supporting leg stands straight or bends slightly, and the other leg kicks up with sole. High-kick to waist level; low-kick to knee level; when to side-kick, upper body tilts and feet up waist. (Picture 32 - Picture 34)

序图32　　　　　序图33　　　　　序图34

（4）铲腿：要求同"踹腿"，唯脚掌朝下，脚尖里扣，脚外侧用力。（序图35、序图36）

Side outer-edge kick: The requirements are the same as "Sole side kick", but sole of the feet down, tiptoe inward, outside of foot using force. (Picture 35, Picture 36)

2. 直摆性腿法　Straight Leg Techniques

（1）正踢腿：支撑腿伸直，全脚掌着地。另一腿膝部挺直，脚尖勾起前踢，接近前额，动作要轻快有力，上体保持正直。（序图37、序图38）

Kick up forward: The supporting leg stands straight with the whole foot touches the ground. The other knee of the leg straighten, hooking foot kicks forward near to forehead, swift and powerful, upper body maintains upright. (Picture 37, Picture 38)

序图35

序图36

序图37

序图38

序图39

序图40

序图41

序图42

（2）里合腿：支撑腿自然伸直，全脚掌着地，另一腿从体侧踢起经面前向里作扇面摆动落下。其他同"正踢腿"。（序图39~序图41）

Inside kick: The supporting leg straight naturally and full foot touches the ground, the other leg kicks up and swings to land like a fan, other action as "Kick up forward". (Picture 39 - Picture 41)

（3）外摆腿：同"里合腿"，唯摆动方向相反。（序图42~序图44）

Outside kick: As "Inside kick" except for the opposite direction.
(Picture 42 - Picture 44)

3. 击响性腿法　Hit Sound Leg Techniques

（1）单拍脚：支撑腿伸直，另一腿脚面绷平向上弹踢；同侧手迎拍脚面，击拍要准确响亮。（序图45、序图46）

Single slap foot: The supporting leg is straight and the other's foot-face straight to kick up; the hand of the same side slaps the foot-face, accurately and loudly. (Picture 45, Picture 46)

（2）斜拍脚（十字拍脚）：同"单拍脚"，唯用异侧手迎拍脚面。

Cross-slap foot: As "Single slap foot", but use the other hand to slap foot-face.

序图43

序图44

序图45

序图46

序图47

（3）里合拍脚：一腿做里合脚动作，脚掌内扣；异侧手在额前去拍脚掌，要准确响亮。（序图47、序图48）

Kick-circle inward and slap foot: A leg kicks inward sole inside; the hand of the other side slaps the sole, accurately and loudly. (Picture 47, Picture 48)

（4）摆莲拍脚：一腿做外摆腿动作，两手在额前依次迎拍脚面，击拍两响，要准确响亮。（序图49～序图51）

Lotus kick: A leg kicks up outward, both hands slap foot in turn, accurately and loudly. (Picture 49 - Picture 51)

序图48

序图49

序图50

序图51

五、平衡
Balances

1. 提膝平衡 Lift Knee Balance

支撑脚直立站稳，上体正直；另一腿在体前屈膝高提近胸，小腿斜垂，脚面绷平内收。（序图52）

Supporting leg stands steadily, body upright. The other knee up to chest with shank oblique inward and foot-face clasps inward. (Picture 52)

序图52

2. 扣腿平衡 Cross-legged Balance

支撑腿屈膝半蹲，另一腿屈膝，脚尖勾起并紧扣于支撑腿膝后。（序图53）

Supporting leg bends to half-squats, bend the other knee with tiptoe hooking straight and leaning on the other knee. (Picture 53)

序图53

3. 仰身平衡 Bending Backward Balance

支撑腿伸直或稍屈站稳，上体后仰接近水平；另一腿伸直举于体前，高于水平，脚面绷平。（序图54）

The supporting leg is straight or bends slightly, the upper body backwards close to level; raise the other leg in front of body in balance higher than level with foot-face stretching tightly. (Picture 54)

序图54

4. 燕式平衡　Swallow Balance

支撑腿伸直站稳，上体前俯，另一腿伸直平衡举于体后，高于水平，脚面绷平。（序图55、序图56）

The supporting leg stands straight, upper body forwards close to level; the other leg is straight in balance backward, higher than hip with foot-face stretching tightly. (Picture 55, Picture 56)

序图55

5. 望月平衡　Looking at Moon Balance

支撑腿伸直或稍屈站稳，另一腿屈膝后上举，脚面绷紧，脚底朝上，上体侧倾并向支撑腿同侧拧腰上翻。（序图57）

The supporting leg stands straight or bends slightly. Bend the other knee and raise it, foot-face stretching tightly with sole upward, upward body pitches sideward. (Picture 57)

序图56

6. 侧搬平衡　Leg up-sideward Balance

支撑腿伸直站稳，另一腿上举过头，两手搬脚。（序图58）

The supporting leg stands steadily, raise the other one over head with hands holding the foot. (Picture 58)

序图57　　　　　序图58

第二节
剑术的基本动作与方法
SWORD TECHNIQUE

一、剑的各部位及其名称
Parts of Sword and Names

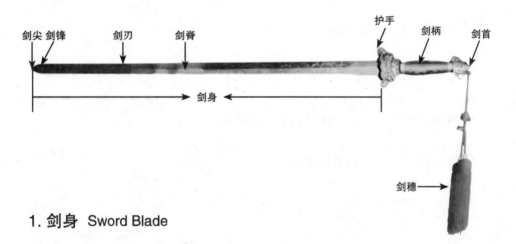

剑尖 剑锋　　　剑刃　　　剑脊　　　　　　　　　　　　　护手　　　剑柄　　　剑首

剑身

剑穗 →

1. 剑身　Sword Blade

剑柄前有刃的部分

The part having edges in front of handle

2. 剑尖　Sword Tip

剑身前端尖锐的部分

The sharp part in the front of blade

3. 剑刃 Side Edges of a Sword

剑身两侧锋利的部分

The two sharp sides of blade

4. 剑锋 The Cutting Edge

剑身前端与剑尖相连的菱形刃

Diamond edge connecting the front part of blade and the tip

5. 剑脊 Spine of Sword

剑身中央突起的部位

Outstanding part in the middle of the blade

6. 护手 Hand Guard

剑身与剑柄间突出的部位

Outstanding part between blade and handle

7. 剑柄 Handle of a Sword

手握的部位

The park that hands hold

8. 剑首 Front Sword

剑柄底端的突出部分

Out standing part sword

8. 剑穗 Sword Tassel

系于剑首后的装饰物

The ornaments tied on the handle

二、握剑的方法
Holding Methods

1. 正握剑 Hold Sword

（序图59）

(Picture 59)

2. 俯握剑 Bending Forward Sword

（序图60）

(Picture 60)

3. 仰握剑 Bending Upward Sword

（序图61）

(Picture 61)

4. 反握剑 Reverse Sword

（序图62）

(Picture 62)

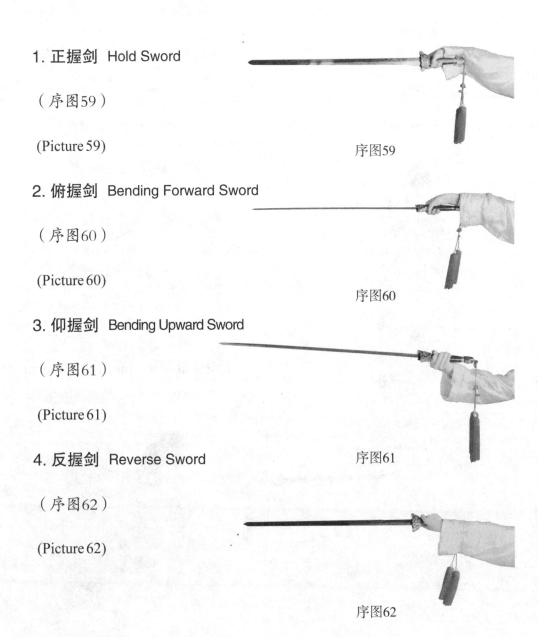

序图59

序图60

序图61

序图62

序图63

1. 持剑礼 Holding Sword Salute

并步直立，左手持剑，
右手立掌，附于左腕，
剑与胸平，目视前方。
（序图63）

Stand at attention, left hand hold the sword with right palm standing on the wrist with sword and chest in the same level. Look ahead. (Picture 63)

2. 持剑 Holding Sword

并步直立，左手持剑，
食指竖直，其余手指，
紧扣护手，右手剑指，
垂于体侧，目视前方。
（序图64）

Stand at attention, left hand holds the sword with index finger straight, and

序图64

序图65

others buttoning hand-guard. Right sword finger hangs down, look ahead. (Picture 64)

3. 刺剑 Thrust Sword

右手正握，由屈到伸，
向前直刺，力达剑尖。
（序图65）

Right hand hold the sword and thrust forward straightly, with power to the tip. (Picture 65)

4. 劈剑 Cut Sword

右手正握，由上直下，
向下劈击，力达剑刃。
（序图66、序图67）

Right hand holds sword, and cut downward with power to the edge. (Picture 66, Picture 67)

序图66

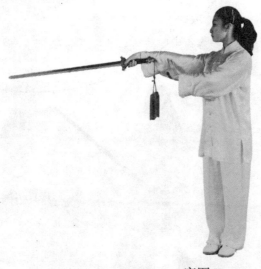

序图67

5. 撩剑 Upper-cut with Sword

右手正握，由下向上，
翻腕上撩，力达剑刃。
（序图68、序图69）

Right hand holds sword, turn over the wrist and cut circle upward with power to the edge. (Picture 68, Picture 69)

6. 挂剑 Parry Sword

右手正握，手臂内旋，
由前向下，向后划弧，
力达剑身。（序图70、序图71）

Right hand holds sword, right arm twists inside and make an arc backward with power to the blade. (Picture 70, Picture 71)

序图68

序图69

序图70

序图71

7. 云剑 Cloud Sword

举剑过顶，朝上横拉，
右腕屈绕，头顶划弧。
(序图72、序图73)

Raise sword over head, draw it horizontally and make an arc over head.
(Picture 72, Picture 73)

8. 抹剑   Slice Horizontally with Sword

右手持剑，翻腕俯握，
弧形回抽，力达剑刃。
（序图74、序图75）

Right hand holds sword, draw back in
arc, with power to the edge. (Picture 74,
Picture 75)

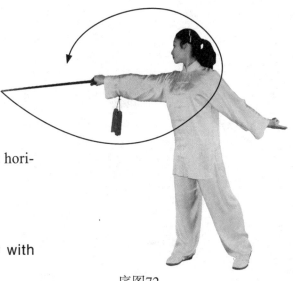

序图72

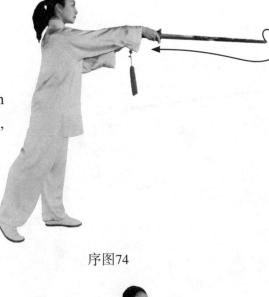

序图74

序图73

序图75

9. 点剑 Point Sword

右手提腕，剑尖下点，
力达剑锋。（序图76）

Lift right wrist and point down with tip, with power to the edge. (Picture 76)

序图76

10. 绞剑 Twist Sword

仰手握剑，右手抖腕，
剑尖划圆。（序图77）

Bending upward sword, quiver right wrist and make circle with tip. (Picture 77)

11. 挑剑
Raise Sword with Straight Arm

右手正握，举剑上挑，
力达剑刃。（序图78、序图79）

Right hand holds sword, raise sword and cut circle upward with power to the edge. (Picture 78, Picture 79)

序图77

序图78

12. 崩剑 Burst Sword

右手正握，沉腕上崩，
力达剑尖。（序图80、序图81）

Right hand holds sword, sink wrist
and burst upward with power to the tip.
(Picture 80, Picture 81)

序图79

序图80

序图81

13. 斩剑 Chop with Sword

右手俯握，平剑横斩，
力达剑身。（序图82、序图83）

Bending forward sword with right hand, then cut horizontally with power to the edge. (Picture 82, Picture 83)

14. 带剑 Withdraw Sword

右手正握，翻腕后拉，
向后收带，力达剑身。
（序图84、序图85）

Right hand holds sword, turn over wrist and pull back with power to the blade. (Picture 84, Picture 85)

序图82

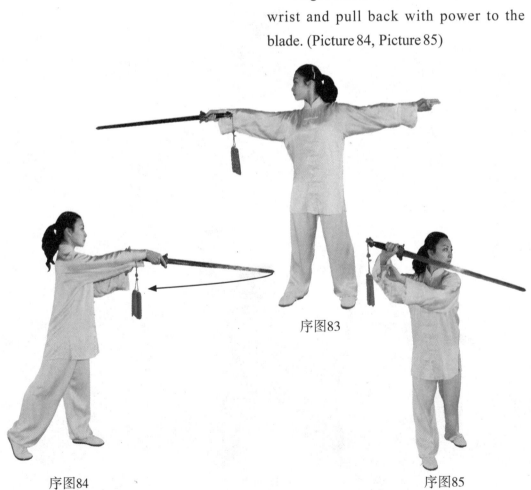

序图83

序图84

序图85

第二章 分解教学与图解

STEP TEACHING AND DIAGRAM

第一节
初级剑术简介
BRIEF INTRODUCTION OF PRIMARY SWORD PLAY

剑，由古代兵器演化而来，是我国武术的四大名器之一，被誉称为"百兵之君"。剑在古时，是作战的武器，有剑锋和两刃，《吴越春秋》卷九和《庄子·说剑篇》都记述了古代击剑的技术和战术，《汉书·艺文志》载有《剑道》38篇，是论述汉以前击剑技术的专著。新中国成立以后，剑术成了剑的演练套路的代称，被列为全国武术比赛项目，增加了各种花法、平衡、翻腾、造型等动作，使剑术有了很大发展。其用法有刺、劈、挂、点、崩、云、抹、穿、压等，在剑法的基础上配以剑指，加上各种步法、步型、跳跃、平衡、旋转等动作构成了剑术的套路。剑术根据练法又分为行剑、势剑、双手剑、长穗剑、双剑、反手剑等。剑术套路繁多，常见的有：青萍剑、武当剑、八卦剑、太极剑、螳螂剑、醉剑、龙形剑等等。

这个套路是中国武术中最基本的剑术套路之一，该套路剑法洒脱，简单易学，是武术的入门套路和必修教材。

本书采用图文教材与影视教材相结合的立体教学手段，并邀请此剑法权威人士进行技术表演和教学示范，保证学习者获取原汁原味的技法传承。

Sword, one of the four famous martial arts, has evolved from ancient weapons. It is called "King of weapons". Sword has a cutting edge and two sides edges. *Wu Yue Chun Qiu* section 9 and *Zhuang Zi·Sword Chapter* all record the ancient fencing technology and tactics, *Han Shu·Yi Wen Zhi* containing 38 sections of sword plays is a special book talking about sword plays before Han dynasty. After People Republic of China was established, sword technics became the name of routine, and is listed as one of national martial arts for competition. It also adds some movements such as various flowers, balance, tumbling, modeling, and so on. Fencing has developed significantly. The main usages are thrust, cut, row, point, burst, wave, daub, penetrate, press and so on. The foundation supported in sword finger, cooperating with all kinds of footwork, infantry-type, jumping, balancing and rotation, makes up the whole routine. According to practicing method, the sword play is divides into Floating Clouds Sword Play, War Sword Play, Double Handed Sword Play, Long-eared Sword Play, Double Sword Play, Fanshou Sword, and so on. Sword routines are many, but the common ones are Qingping Sword, Wudang Sword, Bagua Sword, Taiji Sword, Mantis Sword, Drunk Sword, Dragon Sword, and so on. Sword play is one of the most basic routines in Chinese wushu, it is easy to learn and is a basic and required form.

This book adopts the three-dimensional teaching method of diagram, words and video. The authoritative are invited for technical performance and teaching demonstrations, guaranteeing the learners to gain the real technical method transmission.

第二节
初级剑术动作说明与图解
MOVEMENT EXPLANATIONS AND
DIAGRAMS OF PRIMARY SWORD PLAY

预备式
Preparatory Form

并步直立，左手持剑，
右手剑指，目视前方。
（图1）

Stand at attention, left hand holds sword, right hand forms sword finger (forefinger and middle singer straight, the others bent), look ahead. (Fig 1)

图1

一、起式
Starting Form

1. 两臂上提，右腕内扣，
   头向左转。（图2）

Lift arms, right wrist buckles inside, turn head left. (Fig 2)

图2

图3

2. 左脚横跨，上体左转，
成左弓步，左手持剑，
划弧前指，右手剑指，
向后抬起，两臂同高，
目视前方。（图3）

Left foot steps to the left, upper body turns left to make left bow step. Left hand holds sword, makes an arc and points forward. Right sword finger rises up backward. Two arms in the same level. Look ahead. (Fig 3)

图4

3. 身体左转，右脚上步，
并步直立，左手回摆，
置于体侧，右手剑指，
划弧前伸，目视前方。
（图4）

Turn left, step right foot forward and stand at attention. Left hand sways back and then stays on side of body, right hand with sword finger makes an arc and stretches forward, look ahead. (Fig 4)

图5

4. 右脚撤步，左手持剑，
向前平举，右手后摆，
两臂同高，目视前方。
（图5）

Withdraw right foot, left hand holds sword and raises it horizontally. Right hand sways backward, two arms in the same level. Look ahead. (Fig 5)

5. 重心后移，左脚点地，
   成左虚步，左手后拉，
   右手接剑，目视前方。
   （图6）

Shift weight backward, left foot points the ground to make left empty step. Pull left hand back and the right hand holds sword, look ahead. (Fig 6)

二、弓步刺剑
Thrust Sword in Bow Step

图6

左脚上步，重心前移，
右腿蹬直，成左弓步，
右手持剑，向前直刺，
左手剑指，划弧后指，
目视剑尖。（图7）

Step left foot forward, shift weight forward, right leg kicks straight to make left bow step. Right hand holds sword and thrusts forward straightly. Left sword finger makes an arc and points backward, keep eyes on the tip. (Fig 7)

图7

三、叉步斩剑
Chop with Sword in Crossed Step

图8

右脚上步，上体右转，
左脚点地，成交叉步，
右手持剑，向后平斩，
左手划弧，置于头前，
目视剑尖。（图8）

Step right foot forward, upper body turns right. Left foot points the ground to make crossed step. Right hand holds sword and cuts backward horizontally. Left hand makes an arc and stays in front of head, keep eyes on the tip. (Fig 8)

四、弓步劈剑
Cut with Sword in Bow Step

图9

左脚上步，重心前移，
右腿蹬直，成左弓步，
右手持剑，立剑下劈，
左手划弧，置于头上，
目视剑尖。（图9）

Step left foot forward, shift weight forward, right foot kicks straight to make left bow step. Right hand holds sword and cuts downward. Left hand makes an arc and stays in front of head, keep eyes on the tip. (Fig 9)

五、歇步崩剑
Burst Sword in Cross Legged Step

1. 上体右转，右脚插步，
   脚尖点地，右手下摆，
   左手下落，附于右腕，
   目视剑尖。（图10）

图10

Upper body turns left, make right cross step with the tiptoe on the ground. Right hand sways downward, left hand falls down and stays on the right wrist. Keep eyes on the tip. (Fig 10)

2. 身体右转，双腿全蹲，
   成蹲歇步，右手持剑，
   划弧上崩，力达剑尖，
   左手划弧，置于头上，
   目视剑尖。（图11）

图11

Turn right, bend both legs completely to make cross legged step. Right hand holds sword and burst it upward in arc, with power to the tip. Left hand makes an arc and then stays on the head, keep eyes on the tip. (Fig 11)

六、弓步削剑
Sharpen Sword in Bow Step

1. 身体右转，双腿直立，
   右手下落，掌心向上，
   左手剑指，附于右腕，
   目视剑尖。（图12）

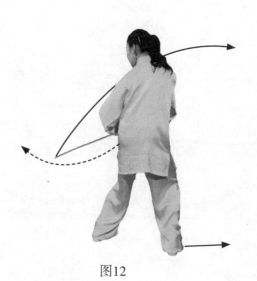

图12

Turn right and stand straight. Right hand falls down with palm upward. Left sword finger stays on the right wrist. Keep eyes on the tip. (Fig 12)

图13

2. 右脚横跨，上体右转，
   重心前移，成右弓步，
   右手持剑，平剑前削，
   左手后拉，目视剑尖。
   （图13）

Right foot steps to the right, upper body turns right, shift weight forward to make right bow step. Right hand holds sword, and cuts forward horizontally. Left hand pulls backward, keep eyes on the tip. (Fig 13)

七、左右挂剑
Parry with Sword Left and Right

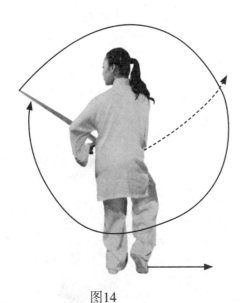

图14

1. 上体左转，重心后移，
   右脚回撤，右手持剑，
   翻腕回挂，左手剑指，
   附于右腕，目视剑尖。
   （图14）

Upper body turns left, shift weight backward, and withdraw right foot. Right hand holds sword, turn over wrist and parry with sword. Left sword finger stays on the right wrist, keep eyes on the tip. (Fig 14)

2. 右脚横跨，右后转身，
成交叉步，右手持剑，
向右挂剑，左手前伸，
目视剑尖。（图15）

Right foot steps to the right, and turn right back to make crossed step. Right hand holds sword and parry with it rightward. Left hand stretches forward, keep eyes on the tip. (Fig 15)

图15

八、叉步压剑
Press Sword in Crossed Step

1. 左脚横跨，两臂平举，
目视右侧。（图16）

Left foot steps to the left, raise both arms horizontally, keep eyes on the right side. (Fig 16)

图16

2. 右脚插步，脚尖点地，
右手持剑，划弧下压，
左手剑指，附于右腕，
目视剑尖。（图17）

Right foot makes crossed step with tiptoe on the ground. Right hand holds and presses down in arc. Left sword finger stays on the right wrist, keep eyes on the tip. (Fig 17)

图17

图18

九、提膝点剑
Lift Knees and Point Sword

1. 右后转身，右手持剑，
   顺势上架，剑指后摆，
   目视右侧。（图18）

Turn right back, right hand holds sword and raises it upward. Left sword finger sways backward, keep eyes on the right side. (Fig 18)

2. 左腿提膝，右腿独立，
   右手持剑，提腕下点，
   左手剑指，架于头上，
   目视剑尖。（图19）

Lift left knee and stand with right leg. Right hand holds sword, lift wrist and point downward, left sword finger rises up and stays on the head, keep eyes on the tip. (Fig 19)

图19

十、并步刺剑
Bring Feet Together and Thrust Sword

1. 左脚落步，上体左转，
   右手持剑，提于胯侧，
   剑指划弧，体前挑起，
   目视前方。（图20）

Left foot falls down, upper body turns left. Right hand holds sword and leaves it at the side of crotch. Sword finger makes an arc and rises up in front of body, look ahead. (Fig 20)

图20

中国武术入门之初级剑术 THE BASIC FORM OF CHINESE WUSHU PRIMARY SWORD PLAY

2. 右脚跟步，并步下蹲，
　持剑前刺，左手剑指，
　附于右腕，目视剑尖。
（图21）

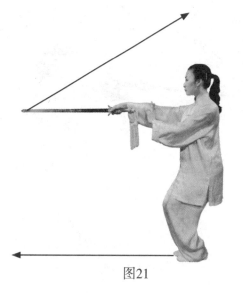

Right foot steps on. Hold feet and bend down. Then thrust forward. Left sword finger stays on the right wrist, keep eyes on the tip. (Fig 21)

图21

十一、弓步挑剑
Raise Sword in Bow Step

右脚上步，左腿蹬直，
成右弓步，右手持剑，
直臂上挑，目视前方。
（图22）

Step right foot forward, left leg kicks straight. Right hand holds sword, raise it with straight arm, look ahead. (Fig 22)

图22

十二、歇步劈剑
Chop with Sword in Cross Legged Step

左脚上步，随即下蹲，
成蹲歇步，右手持剑，
直臂下劈，左手剑指，
附于右腕，目视剑尖。
（图23）

图23

Step left foot forward and bend completely to make cross legged step. Right hand holds sword and chops it with straight arm. Left sword finger stays on the right wrist, keep eyes on the tip. (Fig 23)

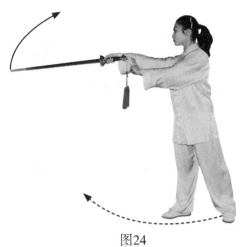

图24

十三、上步截腕
Step Forward and Interrupt Wrist

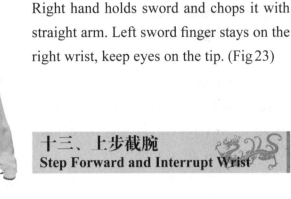

1. 重心上移，右脚上步，右手持剑，剑同肩高，目视前方。（图24）

Shift weight upward, step right foot forward, right hand holds sword, turn over wrist and rise up, look ahead. (Fig 24)

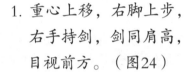

2. 上体不动，左脚上步，脚尖点地，成左虚步，翻腕上架，目视前方。（图25）

图25

Keep upper body still, step left foot forward to make left empty step with tiptoe on the ground, look ahead. (Fig 25)

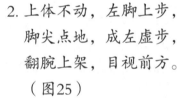

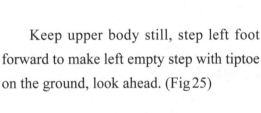

3. 右脚上步，脚尖点地，成右虚步，剑指上举，右手持剑，翻腕上截，目视前方。（图26）

图26

Step right foot forward with tiptoe on the ground to make right empty step. Raise sword finger. Right hand holds sword, turn over wrist and interrupt it upward, look ahead. (Fig 26)

十四、跳步撩剑
Cut in Circle in Jumping Step

1. 右脚上步，上体左转，
   右手持剑，拉回体前，
   左手剑指，附于右腕，
   目视剑尖。（图27）

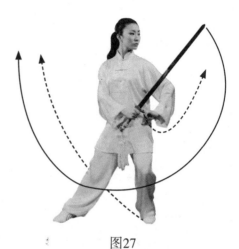

图27

Step right foot forward, upper body turns left, right hand holds sword and draws it back to body. Left sword finger stays on the right wrist, keep eyes on the tip. (Fig 27)

2. 双脚跳起，右腿独立，
   左腿后撩，右手持剑，
   直臂反撩，剑指后撩，
   目视剑尖。（图28）

Jump up and stand with right leg. Left leg cuts in circle backward. Right hand holds sword and cuts in circle back. Sword finger cuts in circle backward, keep eyes on the tip. (Fig 28)

图28

中国武术入门之初级剑术

THE BASIC FORM OF CHINESE WUSHU PRIMARY SWORD PLAY

十五、仆步压剑
Press Sword in Crouch Step

图29

1. 左脚落步，右手持剑，
   环绕一周，目视剑尖。
   （图29）

Left foot falls down, right hand holds sword and wave for a circle, keep eyes on the tip. (Fig 29)

2. 重心后移，左腿全蹲，
   成右仆步，右手持剑，
   后拉下压，左手回拉，
   附于右腕，目视剑尖。
   （图30）

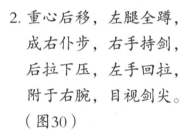

图30

Shift weight backward, bend left leg completely to make right crouch step. Right hand holds sword, pulls it back and presses it down. Left hand pulls back and stays on the right wrist, keep eyes on the tip. (Fig 30)

图31

十六、提膝刺剑
Lift Knee and Thrust Sword

左腿提膝，右腿直立，
持剑平刺，左手上架，
目视剑尖。（图31）

Lift left knee, right leg stands straight, then thrust sword horizontally. Left hand rises up, keep eyes on the tip. (Fig 31)

十七、弓步抹剑
Slice Sword in Bow Step

左脚后落，右腿蹬直，
成左弓步，上体右转，
顺势平抹，力达剑刃，
剑指划弧，体侧上架，
目视前方。（图32）

Fall down left foot backward, right leg kicks straight to make left bow step. Upper body turns right and slice sword with power to the edge. Sword finger makes an arc and rises up at the side of body. Look ahead. (Fig 32)

图32

十八、收式
Closing Form

1. 重心右移，上体右转，
   右手持剑，屈臂回抽，
   左手回拉，附于右腕，
   目视剑尖。（图33）

Shift weight rightward, upper body turns right. Right hand holds sword, then bend arm and withdraw sword. Left hand pulls back and stays on the right wrist. Keep eyes on the tip. (Fig 33)

图33

图34

2. 右脚撤步，并步直立，
   左手接剑，右手剑指，
   划弧下按，两臂下垂，
   目视前方。（图34）

Withdraw right foot and stand at attention. Left hand sword, right hand makes sword finger and presses downward in arc. Both arms hang down, look ahead. (Fig 34)